Subconsciously
SPEAKING

Subconsciously
SPEAKING

YOUR PATH TO PERSONAL POWER

Karen Blaine

authorHOUSE®

AuthorHouse™
1663 Liberty Drive
Bloomington, IN 47403
www.authorhouse.com
Phone: 1-800-839-8640

Published by AuthorHouse   10/16/2012

ISBN: 978-1-4772-8050-8 (e)
ISBN: 978-1-4772-8049-2 (sc)

Contents

Dedication

This book is dedicated to my father, from whom I first learned unconditional love and support.

His indomitable spirit was remarkable as he lost his courageous fight against cancer. I am still inspired by him daily and his presence is always with me.

I also want to thank my husband of over 30 years, Davis, who is an amazing man and my best friend. He is my true inspiration in life, as well as my editor for this book. From my four beautiful children, I have experienced indescribable love and deep delight. I am eternally devoted to Justin, Tristan, Brittara and Whitney.

I also want to thank God for giving me ultimate strength and the ability to believe in myself.

INTRODUCTION

Throughout this book, I have portrayed past memories of my father as he battled cancer. I truly believe hypnotherapy extended his life.

Conversational hypnotherapy and hypnotherapy in general works by allowing the regions deep inside you to activate both the conscious and subconscious mind. This effect is life-altering, as you gradually realize that the deeper levels of your consciousness will confirm the power that you've always possessed.

When you harness these powers, they will work harder for you. 90% of your mind is the subconscious, 10% is the conscious. Too many of us operate in that 10% state of being and rob ourselves of the rich insights the rest of our mind has to offer. By tapping into this hidden area of strength that we all possess, and by drawing from it a new source of energy and positive thinking and being, you can quickly and permanently change the way you handle life.

This book, combined with being open to letting your subconscious free, can help you harness your full potential, your power for greatness and your ability to see beyond the human eye.

FOREWORD

Did you know these nuggets of hypnosis history? These little known hypnosis success stories may just inspire you:

- *Sir Winston Churchill used post hypnotic suggestions to stay refreshed, even though he was up all night during much of World War II*

- *Tiger Woods used hypnosis to help him block out distractions and achieve laser-focus on the golf course*

- *Wolfgang Mozart composed his famous opera "Cosi fan tutte" while in a hypnotic trance*

- *Steve Hooker of Australia won the 2008 Olympic God Medal in pole vaulting after hypnosis helped him visualize winning*

- *Albert Einstein's Theory of Relativity came to him during one of his daily hypnosis sessions*

MORE PROOF OF THE POWER OF THE SUBCONSCIOUS AND CONSCIOUS MIND . . .

YOU ARE INVITED TO DISCOVER HOW TO:

- *Accept the Life you want by looking deep within yourself*

- *Affirm the Power you Possess using your subconscious mind*

- *Achieve amazing Insight to help you attain all of your goals and dreams*

- *Assist your Family, friends and co-workers by helping them use these same techniques*

TURNING DOWN THE VOLUME

How many external feeds or white noise do we receive in one day?

We need to shut off the television, internet, phone, etc. at least a few hours of every day so we can listen to the silence within us.

This is not a drastic life change. It just means reading our paper in silence. That means cooking a meal with silence. Too many of us never have a moment's silence in our day.

How can we hear our important inner voices if we are drowned out by external noise?

How can we make appropriate choices for our lives if we are never clearheaded enough to evaluate them from our own deep inner perspective? Our inner voices communicate with us. These are not the rabid thoughts that invade our mind and can make us crazy with anxiety. These are the soft, inner voices that protect us and make us think before we make a choice in our lives. We need to listen to this voice, and for that we need quiet.

We need to turn down the volume from the external world and listen!

FIGHTING THE GOOD FIGHT

February 2012

Yesterday, I took my father to get his CAT Scan. He has been fighting cancer for four years. It has travelled to his lungs. We have been doing hypnotherapy for a couple of months, at least twice a week. We started doing stress and anxiety relief for him. In the last few weeks, we have been working on eradicating the cancer. He is undergoing radiation at this same time. I am not sure if the CAT Scan is going to show that the cancer tumors are smaller. However, his breathing is so much better. He feels cleaner in the chest and lungs. And, he feels like he has more power, like he has more control.

We have focused on him holding up his right hand, which is the one he favors. We create a white light—made of crystal—into a wand, which he holds in this hand. I tell him how healthy he will be, as he uses his wand to clean out his chest. And, he feels very powerful doing it. Afterward, he feels cleaner, clearer and healthier.

I would love to believe that he has enough power suggestions which are deeply embedded in his mind, body and soul to truly make a difference for him. I do know he is breathing a whole lot better and he is happier and more optimistic. I can live with that!

FERTILIZING OUR MINDS

We all know the stories about the people who "strike it rich" in some way. They find oil or diamonds and they are set for life. We tend to idolize the way people become wealthy.

When we choose to look at our own lives as rich, we believe we too can become just as wealthy.

Let us look at our own lives. Let us use our minds to explore what we have. Let us encompass "gratitude" as our main byword and mantra. Let us live in gratitude and be "grateful" at all times for who and what we are.

One example is the poor farmer, bitter about his barren crop of land. He is jealous of his neighbor for successfully growing tobacco. He carries around tremendous envy and doesn't even plow his own fields. One day he is visited by someone who visualizes the beautiful corn that can be grown on his property. They decide to join together to make the fields a successful farm, supplying corn to the world. Of course, the long story made short is that they become way more successful than the tobacco farmer (who is killing people anyway).

We all know these stories, but we need constant reminders. We have to look around, and open our minds and our souls. We have to go deep inside and listen to our inner voices, which tell us about our treasures. Then, we can go outside and fertilize our own worlds!

A LESSON IN BRAVERY

Some more thoughts about my Dad as he fought cancer. Throughout the cancer, he was incredibly courageous and never panicked, not even for one day. His mind kept him alive as his body failed him. Our minds are simply amazing. From our subconscious to our conscious we have an unbelievable amount of power deep within.

When we worry, we are only hurting ourselves. That is why we must stay present and positive, and know that if we believe all will be well, it will. My Dad trusted his instincts until his last breath. If we adopt a positive attitude, we will present much less anxiety about our present, our past, and our future.

We must use our inner resources at all times. When we remain brave and trust in ourselves, we will always be successful. We are all successes, and we must know that and keep that truth with us at all times. We have the power to make any event a positive experience in some way, even if just to learn from the experience.

IN THE HEAT OF THE NIGHT

Most of us have awoken at 3AM, startled by our dreams. This is when our subconscious mind is extremely active.

Before going to sleep for the night, we might consider reflecting on the just concluded day.
We should tell our brain to resolve the open issues needing attention while we are asleep.
We should reiterate before we fall asleep what we would like to work on during our next day. It might seem funny at first, but we can train our brains to create solutions.

One example I can share is my love for singing. I was a singer before I had children. And I started to sing again after having four children, practicing daily. Within a month of getting back to my old singing ways, my passion strengthened and I began to have musical dreams. Quickly, I put a tape recorder by my bed at night. There are so many songs I have written in my subconscious that never saw the light of day because I couldn't wake myself up to record them-ha! So, now I have my trusty tape recorder and the music my subconscious feeds me is amazing. There is absolutely no way my conscious feeds me is amazing. There is absolutely no way my conscious mind could feel free enough to give me this gift. Think about it and use your dreams to free you, help you, guide you, protect you, and give YOU breakthroughs!!

DOING THE
RIGHT THING

How
many times
do we say to ourselves:
"Oh, I will get to that later."
Something feels like it
isn't very important to us,
so we just don't do it.
At that same moment, our inner
signal or subconscious mind is having
its own moment with us.
We both know it. That inner voice says
"You know you should do it".

*When we start to listen
more to our "inner
voices" and act on
them and DO IT,
we start to feel better.
We accomplish more
externally, too! We feel
better than ever because we
have done the right thing.
We need to trust our inner voices
on a daily basis and know
our subconscious mind is always
there waiting to help us
DO THE RIGHT THING.*

ACCEPTANCE IS KEY

There is a saying I learned in my hypnotherapy class. Our master hypnotherapist would say . . .
WHAT YOU RESIST WILL PERSIST.
WHAT YOU ACCEPT WILL TRANSFORM!
Our conscious minds protect us from harm, but they can also prevent us from absorbing critical information that can prevent us from becoming our "best" version of ourselves. In comparison, our unconscious mind readily accepts vasts amounts of information, in an attempt to help us reach our full potential.

While it's no easy task, we need to unlock our subconscious mind and allow it to work with our conscious. This requires acceptance. Once we accept that sometimes we need to relax, and let our subconscious help guide us, we CAN transform ourselves and our actions. There are times in our lives when we should actually say, "subconscious, help me out" and then do some self-hypnosis.

When we know we are being resistant and it is making us too critical, resentful or pessimistic, that is the time we need to bypass our logical brain which is actually speaking too loudly to us.

We need to say aloud to ourselves that we "accept" what is meant to be. When we believe what we say, our attitude will automatically become positive.

INTERNAL RESPONSES TO AN EXTERNAL WORLD

When my four children were growing up, I used to say I wasn't the greatest cook. Hopefully that has changed and I can now say it is a passion of mine.

During their childhoods, my expression was that: "I cooked their insides" on a daily basis. Instead of asking them if they ate their vegetables today, I asked them how their day was. By "insides," I wanted them to explain how they felt about themselves. What was the best thing about their day? What was the worst thing about their day?

We would spend half an hour together—each one individually—just downloading. I called it self-esteem "talk". I wanted to make sure each child was confident. I felt that, whatever was happening in the world, and with their lives in particular, I wanted them to feel in control of themselves, and their internal value. Then, their behavior and responses would adjust to the external world, accordingly.

I think it worked to a large degree. To this day, I am incredibly proud of my kids.

This inner view of the world should be positive and can help take the sting out of the real life troubles and dilemmas. If we stay positive and believe in ourselves, we can help others and our communities. The very best position we can take is powerful, strong, productive and positive.

LISTENING TO OUR SUBCONSCIOUS MIND

Regardless of what the world around you tells you, you are good enough just being yourself.

Everyone questions him or her self all the time. The moment we start to fear and worry about whether we are good enough is the moment when we aren't being true to ourselves. When we are just ourselves and listen to our subconscious, we are 'good enough'. This is when we have to trust our own body, mind and soul.

The key is to listen to our subconscious mind and know that we are good enough just being our natural selves, and we will succeed in whatever we set out to do. We ARE good enough, powerful enough—JUST ENOUGH—when we draw from our own resources. And when we do, we find we are just perfect—and definitely "good enough".

11

HAVING A PLAN OF ACTION (P.O.A.)

Staying positive is one of the secrets to our own well-being. When life becomes challenging, we need to believe in ourselves. We need to have a P.O.A., plan of action, to keep us in an optimistic state of being.

For every problem there is some solution and/or resolution. When we believe this, it will diminish a lot of the angst we all share. Whether we or a loved one is having a health issue, or a financial hardship, etc., we need to know that we can conquer our challenges. One way to keep life from getting us down is to keep some perspective: on ourselves, our situations, and the universe. Oftentimes a soft sense of humor can help alleviate some of our stress. What is your plan of action?

If you're fighting cancer, like my dad, you can have surgery. If the surgery doesn't work or isn't applicable for you, you can have chemotherapy and radiation. If that doesn't work, you try alternative therapies. The point is you must have a plan at all times. At no point in life do we give up while we're suffering.

BAD HABITS—WE ALL HAVE THEM

We all have that one weakness. Even little things, like excessive consumption of chocolate, coffee—even gum—can turn into a habit rather than a necessity. We just can't seem to break it, however insignificant may seem. But if it troubles you, it's pretty significant. We might say to ourselves that we won't have that piece of apple pie at 8PM one night. We really don't intend to sabotage ourselves, truly. But, we have the piece of apple pie anyway. As soon as we have the feeling, it becomes a thought and then an action. This "network" is structured by the brain.

With hypnotherapy, we can break those rigid and resistant mental barriers. We can be so stubborn!

{ *We cannot go right in through the front door of our brain. We must sidestep our habit with a memorable idea that will buffer, help and protect our good intentions. That way, those good intentions can change this "network" and help break these annoying habits and help us make this change.* }

MAKING
HYPNOTIC
THOUGHTS WORK

It is essential to surround ourselves with healthy, positive, encouraging, uplifting friends, family and even strangers, whenever we can. There are numerous inputs coming at us from everywhere: television to newspapers to other negative influences. It is our choice as to which inputs have a positive impact on our lives.

Negative people or environments can create deep subliminal damage. Such damage represents a bad mental state, about which we may have no awareness.

We must pay attention to the various inputs that affect us. We need to stop and listen to our conscious and subconscious mind for a few minutes a day. Then, we have to think about the effects these inputs are having on our emotions and behavior. By simply being aware, we will make healthier choices.

There are times it is impossible to avoid a negative input. But acknowledging to ourselves that this is what is happening, and choosing how to respond to the input, is a huge step in stopping self-defeating behavior. The more we are aware, the less effect the negative input will have on our lives. And remember, the more we surround ourselves with positive inputs, the more we grow and create additional happiness and self-confidence in our lives.

FOLLOWING *OUR* PATH

A ●

We all see shining lights in our path that are there to guide us.

We all hear voices from friends and strangers that seem to beckon us to follow our own destiny.

We must not allow fear or lack of a personal resolve to take us away from our truths.

We know if we listen carefully, we can trust those who would surely help us to follow along a positive path.

We know if we decide to make ourselves significant, then we will be.

We all know we have much to offer to the universe!

We have to slow down, listen, and never accept anything close to defeat.

To stop following our path mean we are no longer giving our own unique gift and imprint to the world.

So, we must follow our own individual paths and be open to sharing our gifts with the world.

All of the time.

All through the doubt.

We will achieve!

B ●

15

INTERNAL PROGRAMMING

We have been programmed by our parents since birth in subliminal and overt ways. We are also continually affected by our community and culture in general.

Each of us process these stimuli in a very deep, personal way; sometimes we are not even aware of the programming. Even as adults we continue to believe in this programming. Some of us are more adept at surviving when we are thrown into negative experiences than others. But, each of us has the capability to overthrow the bad imprints that threaten to bring us down.

We can change any negative inner programming by understanding and changing the way we perceive our current situations. Each time we want to make a judgment, we need to pause and reflect on what we are thinking and feeling. If we are using the any negative programming, we must adjust and change that framework into a positive way of looking at a situation.

It is interesting that some of us have had very positive programming and are still negative in our thought processes. Interesting wiring, eh? And then there are those that are motivated by their positive conditioning to lead stellar lives.

We who tend to be negative must also work hard to change the programming that has helped us in our survival, but in reality, has only been there to hurt us. Being aware will help us break down these negatives and turn them into positives.

CONSIDERING OUR SOURCE

 It's very important when we are working with a business associate, friend or even family member to consider his/her reaction to what we are discussing. Empathy and its importance in a situation cannot be overstated. We have a tendency to look past the empathy and look only at our reaction to an event, and respond accordingly.

Our success, both professional and otherwise, depends on our ability to listen. We can prepare in our minds a scenario solely dependent on another's reactions and feelings. With this mental preparation, we are able to reflect on our own values in a more thoughtful way.

We can imagine what others say, and how they feel, and absorb it in order to better understand their needs. It doesn't mean we necessarily have to follow along with everything one is saying. But we will be surprised by how much we can learn from everyone by looking at the world from their perspective. We can help others and ourselves when we really "hear" someone!

GOING TO SLEEP

Sometimes we can program our minds before we go to sleep to sharpen our subconscious activity and allow for creative and productive thoughts.

Sometimes, though, we simply need a fantastic night's sleep, where dreaming purifies us and regenerates us. These are the times we want to clear our mind before going to sleep. These are the times we want to take five minutes before sleep to do some deep breathing and focus ONLY on breathing. If we are successful in this, all our cares diminish and all thoughts of tomorrow can be reduced into one feeling of peace, contentment and relaxation. Then, we enter the sleep state at the deepest levels, and experience that healthy, quality nightlong sleep which replenishes our physical bodies and our soul.

Many people have difficulty falling asleep. That is why it is so important to "prepare" for the night. For some, it is more like an hour of relaxation. That includes a warm bath, light stretching, soft music, or whatever relaxes us. Deep sleep is critical.

We then wake up so refreshed to face the day!

FEELING OUR PAIN

When we get hurt by the reactions of others, our first reaction is to deny our pain. We know that if we feel too deeply, it will incapacitate us. So we choose to avoid those feelings. But the opposite is true. We need to experience the pain to understand it and let go of it.

We need a time and place to release our sorrows. We need a person in our lives to whom we can divulge our own truths, whatever they are. If we hold our emotions inside, including our anxiety, worry, etc., and don't let them out, we will have physical problems in addition to our emotional ones.

> We must stop trying to gloss over our disappointment and feelings of loss like they are not real. Often times they are very real. We need to share our deepest sadness about those feelings. Allowing these feelings to reach the light is necessary for our health and survival!

The positive part about allowing ourselves to go "negative" is we can express ourselves. And, later we will actually become more "positive". It is impossible for us to heal if we don't "let it out"! So, we must, even if it seems impossible, shout/cry/talk . . . whatever it takes. Then, we can smile and laugh again.

THE EYES HAVE IT

There is an expression which says that the "eyes are the windows to the soul." When we look into another person's eyes, we can see the depth of their being. There are good liars who work hard to shield or divert their eyes from telling the truth, but most of us are not good liars!

The most important way for us to communicate with another person is to look into their eyes. For us hypnotherapists, it is a critical way to get directly into one's subconscious. One time in a class, our assignment was to stare into our partner's eyes without saying a word for thirty minutes. This was so fascinating to us. We ranged from a soft thought, to tiring, to crying, to laughing, to learning, and more. After the exercise, my partner and I had formed a bond (without EVER saying a word)!

We must use our eyes and look into the eyes of others and glean meaning from them. When we truly look at another person, they feel us listening to them. Try the exercise of really looking into other people's eyes and see how connected you feel.

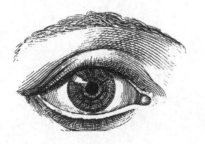 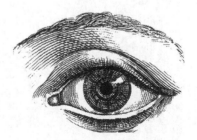

CARING WHAT THEY SAY

" Sometimes, I think the best part about getting older is getting wiser: worrying less about what others say. If we make mistakes, which we will, we know we will learn from them. If they are held against us, then we need to decide to stop listening to people who only want to believe the worst.

We need to believe what we know is true to us (our truth). If we have altered our behavior to satisfy someone else's beliefs, we have empowered that person. There will always be people who want to gossip and "take us down". There will always be people who don't "love us", even though a part of us wants everyone to like us.

The key is to listen to those who want to encourage and enrich us; those, who allow us our independent thoughts. Most importantly, we should ignore others who would tear us down and make us feel less than. It is easy enough to beat ourselves up. We need not worry about the "others" who would only add to our fears about being not good enough.

We know we have to stop "caring what others say". And, when we do, we will live a more mature and happier life! "

FINDING THOSE PEARLS

Trapped within us are oyster shells with our own precious pearls.

We have to access them. By fishing for them, and finding them like a protected species, we can nurture and cherish them.

We all have such unique gifts that we forget. Then, we recognize something we have done well, and reflect on those gifts.

We should open our shell and use the pearls to make our "necklace", and enhance our internal gems.

We must always remember that there are unlimited numbers of pearls within us . . . we are an ocean of untapped truths!

We must do our best to find our pearls, and use them as wisely as possible.

Only then, will we be making the most out of our lives and finding the magic within!

WHEN DARKNESS FALLS

How many times have we experienced feelings where we want to bury our heads (not to mention our hearts) in our hands and just weep!

The darkness in our fuzzy brain and soul feels like it will last forever.

The powerful presence of our beautiful subconscious blankets us. We are not even aware of it. That subconscious allows us to grieve. That subconscious knows we are abandoning ourselves to our heartache. And, that subconscious knows there is a time to emerge out of it.

Our subconscious will help us bounce back and survive. Our subconscious will help us to feel the breeze again, and even to thrive.

Our subconscious is where our faith is the most tightly held and divined. We should always be able to access our subconscious mind. We should be able to go between the conscious and the subconscious to protect us and to guild us.

When darkness falls, we can allow it to help us endure for those moments. We can absorb the hit. But we have to know that for all of the darkest moments, there will be light. The light will start faint at first, but then grow brighter and brighter.

The light will shine!

HIDDEN TREASURES

We have so many hidden treasures locked away in the recesses of our subconscious mind. We have to call them forward. Very different than our pearls of delight, these treasures are stored memories. These are memories of situations we were in which we too often forget. We sublimate them. We should recall them and bring them into the conscious, to help us to grow from them.

These locked, learning mysteries have brought us joy and sorrow, tears and laughter. We can use these to help us every day, in every way.

We must not be afraid to access these hidden treasures, as they "hold many keys" to our growth.

We must take the treasure into the conscious and examine it, to learn from it. How can we utilize our treasures in such a way as to benefit us in the here and now?

We will know the answer. It is within each of us. The smile of a stranger from years past who made us feel wonderful; that recall may help us feel fulfilled, when we might otherwise feel lonely. We can and must use our hidden treasures to find more treasures, and happiness.

WALKING IN YOSEMITE

When we love someone, we want them to find a peaceful, serene place where they are protected, loved and nourished.

This truly is the last thought about my Dad. In his last weeks of life, he was at home under hospice care. He had a lot of love around him, and had a light in his eyes and his smile. He was a beautiful man!

On many occasion, we would "walk" in Yosemite. Yosemite was one of his favorite nature places.

When I took his hands and transformed healing energy from my body to his, we would be ready for the walk.

Often we would find ourselves in the middle of the forest, where there would b e a waterfall.

My point about this visualization and meditation is that two people can share a deep feeling of peace and enjoyment together by a meeting of the minds.

We were not doing hypnotherapy during these times. We were just two people who loved each other, and loved Yosemite. I bring this up because we should focus on our favorite places, like nature spots, and do our own visualizations. We should enjoy our own visits to our favorite destinations. It is peaceful, calming and fun.

HAPPY HYPNOTIC THOUGHTS

Hypnotic thoughts are intended to help make us think, laugh, reflect, cry, challenge ourselves, learn, love a little more, try a little harder, and dig a little deeper.

Hopefully, they will do that. They will encourage us to open up more, to allow ourselves the opportunity to truly listen to our voices, and to hear our silences from deep within.

We can dance at the full moon. We can read a literary classic in a foreign language (or not)! We can believe in ourselves. In every way with every day. When we cherish the day, we honor ourselves and others, when we live in gratitude for all that we have and minimize what we think we don't, we grow and succeed beyond our wildest dreams! Love is still the ultimate word!

UNDERDOG

There is a "Rocky" feeling in all of us! Most of us have a soft spot for people who achieve when the "deck" is stacked against them. We know that it is harder to succeed when we have physical or mental disabilities or come from many disadvantages. It is no coincidence that the most popular movies involve a hero who defies all odds to succeed.

We truly want the good guys to win and we want to help those less fortunate. These feelings are part of our innate human nature!

We also feel some kinship with the underdog, since each of us has been an "underdog" in certain situations. We know it is okay to root for the Lakers or the Celtics, or teams that are almost always at the top of their games. If we only wanted the underdog to succeed, that might be a little unusual.

The good thing, though, is our affinity for those who capture our imagination when they achieve, a la Jeremy Lin (an almost overlooked basketball player who suddenly reached superstardom). There is an innate commonality among us all that believes we, too, can come from behind.

We should all be happy that we believe in coming from behind to take the race and win!

THE CYCLE OF LIFE

Life takes on purpose and meaning with its changes and cycles. One crowning event begins as another ends. In the same week that my son got engaged, my father passed away. The cycle of life is constantly rotating.

When we take the time to fully participate in the changes that occur, and try to adjust ourselves to their realities, we can grow with them. We can own the hurt and the happiness, the fear and the expectations. We can accept that change will and does occur. We can knowingly realize that there will be births, deaths and everything in between.

We know this still doesn't erase what we truly feel about such changes. They can seem scary, even the good changes. For what will happen in the future? But, it does help somewhat to know that this earth and our time here is about our cycles and they will happen to us whether we like it or not. So we might as well do our best to embrace these cycles of life. Feel the pain and sadness, and relish the joys and the happiness.

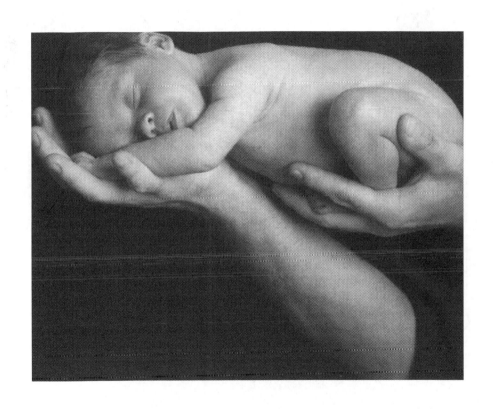

we are less inclined to remain innocent about love. We can become very disillusioned and allow bitterness to rob us of our true desire to love very powerfully.

To love and feel the pain of love is far greater than never having loved at all. At least that is what we have been told.

And we have to believe it is true. Love is almost as important as the air we breathe. Love keeps us alive when we are ill and ready for death. Knowing we are loved allows us to face each day with courage and with grace. Knowing we love fills our heart with warmth and positive energy.

Many people live happy lives without love. In terms of true survival, we cannot live without food and water. But we can't [unable to read]

UNCONDITIONAL LOVE

And so we love! We have animals or CHILDREN, and we learn what true, unconditional love feels like! There is so much depth to our love that we feel powerful (or powerless) to explain in words how wonderful love is. There is a physical sensation at times that tells us how beautiful is this feeling.

And so we live! We live without expectations, without a desire for a "return on love investment". We just love! How tremendous this feeling can be. And the feeling grows deeper the more we realize that there is no agenda to it. We don't need any reciprocity because we have been given our reward just by virtue of our happiness with the ones we love.

And so we grow! And how we grow! The more we see our love does not need to be defined, it just is, the wiser we become. We can understand all of the silly things others do for love. We would and could do it ourselves. How lucky we are to have the opportunity to enjoy this unconditional love!

And so we believe! For as long as we believe, we can have unconditional love. It is like magic nectar for us. We can "breathe in" our delight and there isn't anyone or anything that can take our love away!

How lucky we are!

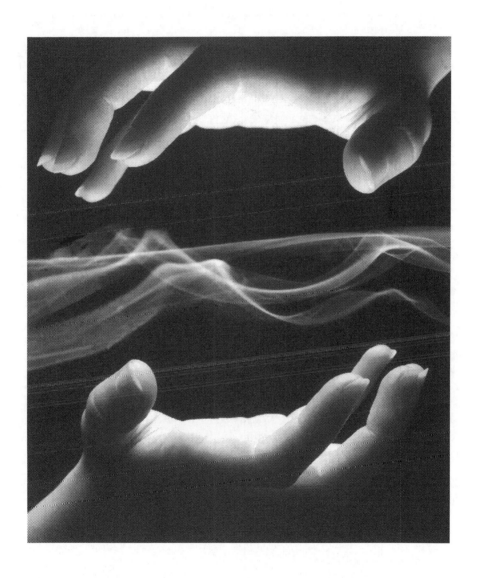

[unable to read] Will this day be a great one that we are proud of? Our mind is already leaping ahead to plan for the best.

Before our mind starts to clutter, we should give ourselves 10 minutes to get centered. Let us enjoy that wonderful feeling when time can be our friend. For 10 minutes, let us not worry about being late to anything. We must still the voice in our head for these minutes to set ourselves up for a fantastic day ahead.

Let us lay here, half-awake and half-asleep, and use our subconscious to give us strength to face the day with surety, and courage. At this time we can, but do not need reflection. To just deep breathe and feel serenity and a sense of peace is the best way to start the day.

Now, after we experience this moment, we know we can start moving with a little more enthusiasm, and a willingness and delight to face the new day and its challenges! ☀

NON-VERBAL COMMUNICATION

My favorite college course was non-verbal communication, because so much more is being said when it is silently communicated.

It is important to allow our subconscious mind to take in our situation, our connections, and how we are appearing to others. If we allow our arms to remain uncrossed and relaxed and we have a large smile that is genuine, others will see us as open to them and sincere. The same is true for them. Our astute subconscious is always working overtime to make sure that what people say is what they really mean. What we see, feel and sense is more often an accurate perception of what is really going on than the actual communication.

If we are aware of these non-verbal gestures, nuances and even "auras", we can distinguish reality from perception. Such a heightened awareness allows us to receive more information, as well as relay more sincerity to others.

But if we are acutely aware of what is "not being said", our understanding of the interaction is far more real and beneficial.

EXPECTATIONS

We all have certain expectations that we believe will be met, or not. Sometimes it almost seems that we are afraid of our own expectations. We think we will let down, or we will let ourselves down.

We have to remember to set our expectations high enough to challenge ourselves, yet realistic enough not to be striving for the impossible.

Expectation can truly get us into trouble. The very word can conjure up fear and insecurity. Too often, we set our self up for disappointment by the very expectations we have created.

We need to tamper down our need to always be rewarded in some way. That need causes unrealistic expectations.

Sometimes, the easiest way to ruin a relationship with our loved ones is when we require them to be a certain way or expect them to handle situations the way "we" would.

Our self-imposed expectations can make us impossible to live with. We need to sift through the choices that we make, have made, and will make, and stop demanding that they be more or less than they are.

Then, our expectations will be realistic and not overwhelming!

THE SMILE WITHIN

We can fix a smile on our face even if we are tired or sad. Others will see us with our smile. From an internal perspective we will start to feel the smile!

There is an old truth: what we show on the outside, we can start to feel on the inside. This means that by wearing a smile we will start to feel like smiling.

As the day continues, we will find that the smile within will begin to illuminate more and more. We will start to feel better and lighter, and have a more positive outlook to our day. It is impossible to be angry and smile at the same time (at least genuinely). And by the end of the day, we will be glad we put on that smile. We plastered it on in the beginning of the day (hopefully most times it is a real smile!). But, even if it is not "real", wearing it for a day will encourage a smile.

Hopefully, tomorrow the smile will come more naturally. For today we helped it along.

LIVING
IN THE NOW

Everyone has heard these expressions: *Live for the Moment. Live in the now and forget the past. It's over. Don't live in the future, it hasn't happened. Be present in the moment, as the moment is happening.*

Most of us have heard these expressions and tried to practice them. Fulfilling these life statements is often difficult because our minds find constant distraction. We almost have to shut down our minds and restart them to focus on the present. In order to focus on the NOW, we must practice. and, as another saying goes, "practice makes perfect."

One approach is an analogy I like to use. Our minds are like a remote control, constantly changing the channel until our brain waves are satisfied. Instead of flipping through those channels, especially "stress" channels, we should stop at a channel for longer than we ordinarily would and look for the good in it.

Living in the NOW is crucial for us to have an incredible life. When we put our ALL into each moment, each act, and what we are currently doing, we are really living!

This practice may not come naturally. But that is all the more reason to hear this same information over and over again.

SOCIALIZATION SKILLS

How often do we interact socially with people, yet feel invisible?

The key to believing we can be successful in social situations is to trust that we have intrinsic value. If we look at another person and make eye contact, it will be hard for them to look away. Thus, we have made a connection with them. Then, we use our smile to help us forge a positive impression; voila, we made our impact and are not invisible.

Of course, there will still be people that don't "give us the time of day". That is not our problem. Likely, they might be too immature, self-centered, or introverted to deal with others. One example would be the young girl in the shop who won't get off her cell phone as she rings up your merchandise. She does not even look at you. That is not our issue. The truth is that we can smile indulgently at her, knowing she will grow up soon enough and learn how to connect with people.

We can use each day to train ourselves to be more sociable. It is important, if only because we are imparting good thoughts and kindness to those with whom we are interacting. They feel good, and better about themselves, and so do we.

INSTANT CONNECTION

One of the keys to establishing a quick, easy and trustworthy connection to a friend, business associate, client, etc. is to tell a personal story. When thinking of the story to relate, obviously we need to consider to whom we are telling the story.

However, this is one surefire way to instantly form a common bond. If we know the other person has children or pets, or likes to ski or go boating, we can call us a similar story from our own lives to which they can relate. For example, we can talk about our ski incident with the horrible weather that had us locked into our cabins. And tell a story around this incident. There will be an instant connection, and most people will be happy that they have something in common with us.

We all have personal stories from which we can draw. When we try to find a common ground that with someone else, they will feel more comfortable with us, hopefully, feel like we are more trustworthy.

In turn, chances are good they will tell us a story about a common or related theme and the relationship rapport is established.

This is a very special way to start a relationship with another person.

AND SOCRATES SPEAKS

 I learned a lot of wonderful tools about human behavior from my master hypnotherapist. One important tool that I will share is mastering the "ancient art" of the Socratic Method of hypnotic questioning. This method has been proven successful over centuries.

Developed by the ancient Greek philosopher Socrates around 450 BC, this method can break down resistance, cynicism, and skepticism among other barriers. It can help us to help others. Accordingly, it has been found in Shakespeare's works and was extremely important to Freud, among other sources.

When dealing with others, at times we want to answer a question with another question. We will then use those questions to find out about the other person's values and beliefs. This helps us to understand their way of thinking. We can then frame our next question to help them decide what they might like us to share with them more directly.

Lastly, knowing many people are distrusting of our motivations and are hesitant to engage with us, we can frame our questions to help overcome that resistance. Then, we keep them invested in us and can direct the conversation to convince others of our sincerity. Hopefully we will be effective in helping them, or even just helping them share.

SUBCONSCIOUSLY SPEAKING

We can help ourselves heal through the magic of communicating with ourselves. That is what I call 'subconsciously speaking.' When we tell ourselves on a deeper level how fantastic we are, then we give ourselves permission to believe it.

Every time we start to think negative thoughts then it is immediately time for us to allow our subconscious to speak. We can heal ourselves with our words. When we subconsciously speak, we negate all of the negative imprints we have heard throughout our lives that have made us doubt ourselves. Then, we place deep in our minds positive words that will translate into positive action.

We can subconsciously tell ourselves that failure is not an option. We can be brave and courageous. We can use our instincts and trust them. There are so many wonderful things we can do to help ourselves when we subconsciously speak.

THE LANGUAGE OF THOUGHT

The thoughts we have form our very own language. That is why it is so important to make those thoughts amazing. When we use our "thought language" to believe that "life is good", we form our own internal language to help us.

We can consciously use our own words and place them into our subconscious to give us our own positive spin on life. We cannot allow negative "thought traps" to hurt ourselves. This is our opportunity to implant words to help us enjoy life to its fullest!

We can pick some of our favorite words that mean something to us individually. We all have some words that mean something special to us. We should use them to help with our thoughts, such as acceptance, confidence, and well-being. Whatever words that we choose to use become our language of thought.

AaBbCcDd
AaBbCcDd
AaBbCcDd

Isn't it fascinating to know we have our own unique language? Isn't it wonderful to know our special language helps us to enrich our lives?

THOUGHT TRAPS

When we use our language of thought, we implant positive concepts into our minds. This language helps us avoid negative thought traps. Those traps might be a negative word association. When that happens, we must always switch our language. We need to say the words, "I am SO good, just as I am".

Instead of saying "I am NOT (fill in the blanks . . . rich enough, thin enough, cool enough, etc.)", we need to say "I am SO SO good enough just as I am".

We can help ourselves with our language of thought. And we can also hurt ourselves. The choice is always up to us. We must be careful of these thought traps in our language, and make sure we are helping ourselves at all times. we should always know how important we are to this world and our planet. We should always know that we deserve an enriched and beautiful life. When we substantiate ourselves with the positive language and guard against negativity in our thoughts, we can achieve anything.

POWER WORDS

Power words, when used in a certain way, help us emphasize to others the significance of what we are trying to tell them. Examples of power words are: BECAUSE, AND, AS SOON AS, WHICH MEANS, and WHEN. Most people don't even realize these are power words, but they are. They grab other people's attention. Used at the appropriate time, these words redirect our conscious mind to comprehend the conversation (or whatever follows) on a deeper level. They are words that help to tell a cohesive and well-understood story.

*There are alternatives to power words that are almost as impactful, in slightly different ways. Some of these are: **Be Aware, Realize, Think, Remember, Think Back or Forward, Look, Feel, See, Consider, Notice, Recall, Imagine, Pretend and Focus On.***

The words shift others' attention and open our minds. They make others focus on the bigger picture. Then, the meaningful ideas become clearer.

Thus, using special words help us to learn more, mostly by refocusing the brain to accept the message.

THE POWER OF PASSION

Passion can be an amazing and powerful emotion! It allows us to love more deeply and fully. It allows us to bring more intensity to our families, careers and hobbies. It awakens in us the ability to apply our talents in a more creative and fulfilling manner. We can harness our passion for greatness and can achieve to an even greater ideal. Many of us are almost afraid to release our passions. We feel it can harm us in some way, or show us as too ego-centric. We truly need to believe that our passion can feed us like fuel, like food is to our bodies.

Without passion, we are just living. With passion, we are completely living! We need to trust in our passion, knowing that we can take ourselves to a more powerful level when we utilize these wonderful emotions. And, most people are energized by and connected to us when we share and display our passions. As long as we are not pushing our passions onto others to the extent of appearing self-righteous, others will connect to our passions.

As we trust our passions, we feel more fully alive, awake and invested in our lives. We can be comforted and joyous that we feel this way. We need to remember at all times it is great that we can take our lives to an entirely new level just by relying on this amazing emotion.

We need to allow ourselves to be free and believe that passion can propel us to a greater investment in ourselves and the world. What that means is we can use two exclamation points (!!) instead of one (!) What a wonderful world in which to live!!

OPENING
OUR MINDS

We need to understand how important it is to remain open and flexible to what life bestows upon us. Being flexible allows us to relax, deal with pressure, and not take things so personally.

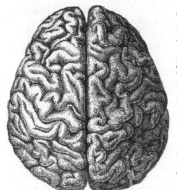

When we tell ourselves that some areas of our life are not "perfect", at least not right now, we are giving ourselves permission to be fine. By opening our minds to changes that occur, we can "roll with the punches" far more easily. We can see that everything will turn out fine, even if we hadn't intended to go in this or that direction.

Another unintended result of being open is to more fully enjoy the changes in the road. We can plan on going skiing in a certain area and find out there is no snow. So, we go to the ocean instead and have a good time. We can see how change benefits our lives, which may not happen if we are not open to it.

By opening our minds, we learn and grow in so many ways. When we are fixed, we are actually perpetuating our own negativity. On the other hand, the fullness and richness of life becomes more obvious to us every time we allow ourselves to relax and enjoy what the world has to offer us, even when it doesn't go according to our plan!

OPENING OUR HEARTS

When we open our hearts, much like opening our minds, we have the capacity to stretch our joy a thousand-fold. We can feel love on such a deep level. There is no limit to our love. For so many of us, we feel if we love in one way, we cannot love in another way, as well. We logically know that is not true, but we prevent ourselves from opening our hearts to all the love we can receive.

We can be "in love" with nature, with our job, our mate, our children, and the list goes on and on. The more we allow ourselves to love and be fully open and participate in the connections, the more our heart muscles stretch, expand and complete our lives and ourselves. How lucky we are to have this opportunity.

Then, we can be connected to the world in every way! By not limiting ourselves to our own "backyard love", but allowing the world to give us all the love we can receive, we are transporting ourselves into so much more happiness. Our hearts then feel full and happy. What we give to others, when it comes from the heart, helps them and helps us in more ways than we can imagine. We need to always be open to enriching our lives by allowing love to enter our hearts and souls, and not being afraid of it. Then, we will allow a world that is so full that we cannot be empty, afraid or lonely. Our hearts will sing in gratitude, and our pride will be immeasurable!

OWNING OUR AMBITION

Being ambitious is wonderful. When we are ambitious, it means we want to achieve so much in our lives. We have plans, goals and dreams to help ourselves, and hopefully to enrich our world.

We can give ourselves a "blueprint" for our goals, and then follow it and be proud of our ambition. If our ambition is to have a family and raise our children well, or to win a Nobel peace prize, planning for it will make it true for us.

We tell ourselves at times that being ambitious can come at the cost of losing our sincerity. We think it may appear too egotistical to others. That is not true, and those kind of negative thought patterns prevent us from doing our best in the world.

We should think of our ambition as the ability to do a phenomenal job here on Earth. We can produce a legacy that will last long after we are gone. We should think of our ambition as a propeller that can help us to fly. We need to believe that being ambitious helps us to take risks in order to succeed. We should trust that our ambition can be used properly and truthfully, and can help us to help the world in our own very special way.

A SHOCKING
STORY
(the Cycle of Life—Part II)

Today, I was taking out the trash when I saw a dead, half-eaten deer that appeared to be pregnant. To say I was shocked is an understatement. families of deer live in my development, and they have adapted well to the humans. In many ways, I have "watched out for them". We have such beautiful mountains and sky here. However, all is not perfect in paradise.

We have coyotes here in abundance; they are always running in packs and eating small animals such as dogs. I have two small Maltese dogs, which are never in our yard alone. And, we walk them during daylight hours. Anyhow, as I saw this beautiful (but dead) deer, many thoughts went through my mind.

The first thing I did was call my Dad, who was at the end of his life. Of course, it makes you think about the cycle of life. This is the way of nature: the purpose, the plan! This plan has many dimensions, and can seem confusing and outright terrifying. When I saw the deer, I became afraid about life itself. Then, I thought that there is a reason coyotes are here (there must be) and they need to eat. We believe there is a master plan for the universe. Still, how sad it must be for the family of the deer and for those of us alive who continue on.

So, armed with my subconscious strength, I stopped being shocked. I went to gratitude for all that I had enjoyed with the deer. I empathized with the rest of the family of deer, and hoped they wouldn't leave the development. And, of course, I thought of my own father, with my eternal gratitude for all of the life I have had with him!

THE "KAREN" SHOW
(A Metaphor for Life)

Our lives are amazing because we can script them any way we choose. We have a script for our lives. We can call it The "insert our name" Show, and make it what we want.

Now, on this day, or in this moment, we can add a chapter or change a chapter. We are the writer, creator, producer of The "our name" Show. We are in control of our own show; we are in mastery!

We can rewrite the script, add to the script, whatever we like. We have to remember this metaphor at all times. We are not the victim, we are the victor of life. We choose our story, our script. We can have a beautiful show if we say it is so.

Assume that our lives (that we want to make better) have been written in pencil. We can erase it and write anew. We can do this in our OWN handwriting with our OWN pen, creating even more of our own life. We must remember we are the master of our destiny. We can let go of negatives, stress, old habits, and unhealthy associations. They are no longer relevant to us.

We are once again, the creator, producer and writer of The "our name" Show, which is truly wonderful.

EFFECTIVE PERSUASION

There is an old saying that we all know. "You can catch more flies with honey than with vinegar".

Sometimes we run into resistance to our ideas. This is the time we need to learn how to influence others with gentle persuasion, and not brute force. It is also the time to reflect on our ideas to ensure they are meritorious and not just based on a selfish personal agenda. Nobody reacts well to being hit over the head with our thoughts.

Everyone has a positive reaction when they think it is a mutual idea and will benefit them. We always need to remember to use our words wisely and soften our statements.

When we help people to understand the WHY *of what they are choosing to do (or not do), they usually* WANT *to concur with us. Using the tools of collaboration to "champion" our "rational" position, we most often will receive acceptance from others.*

We often need to count to ten before speaking our thoughts and our mind, most especially when we are angry. By the time we get to ten, we have softened our thoughts. When, we will be listened to in a much more sympathetic way. Others will be much more amenable to making a change. Our suggestions will be their suggestions. We will be happy because the change will come from both of us.

FACING OUR CHALLENGES
(and Winning)

We have read about so many people who have overcome all odds to succeed. How do they do it? Where do they get such fortitude? We know that they conquer their challenges and prevail. We can all do it. We know people who have overcome physical and health problems, financial problems, setbacks, and hardships, and became rich and successful beyond measure. Why do they achieve so much when they have been dealt such a losing hand in life?

We can face our own challenges and win. We need to believe we can succeed. To triumph we need to believe in ourselves. We need to know that as long as we can take a breath, we can overcome our obstacles. Life is never a smooth journey, even for those people that appear to have the ideal existence without significant obstacles. Every human faces a myriad of issues and problems, often every day. It is our "personal obligation" to create our own destiny.

We need to expect problems, and not become incapacitated by them. We can't even allow ourselves to think we will fail. We will conquer the pitfalls and be stronger than ever.

We will face our challenges with grace, and we will win. We have to believe in ourselves at all times. We have to trust that we have the capabilities to triumph. And then, we will!

OUR CONSCIOUS GATEKEEPER
(Our Mind)

We need our conscious mind to act as a gatekeeper to reign us in when we don't want to access our subconscious. The conscious gives us direction and protects us. Our conscious accesses the subconscious, which helps us process and produce information to the world. We use our conscious to know what to say and when to say it. We have learned so much from our conscious that keeps us safe.

We must trust our conscious mind to integrate with our subconscious. Together, the two keep us growing, learning and accessing. The conscious mind gives us the focus that we need. We can trust the conscious gatekeeper to access only the information that we want to share. How wonderful it is that we have both our subconscious and conscious mind working together!

How perfect it is that we have our conscious gatekeeper there to keep us safe, and our subconscious mind to absorb what we are learning. We truly need both to interact with each other. What is amazing is how instinctively they perform.

WHEN NATURE CALLS

We can pick our favorite place in the world and regularly visualize it. To begin the exercise, we pick our favorite mountains, city, ocean or other location. Then, we can take a few deep breaths, relax and start our visualization.

Here is an example we can use. I love Big Sur, California. Visualizing this scene of certain cliffs is a "heavenly" experience for me. When I picture this place, I can truly relax and self-hypnotize. I am peaceful here. It is also an opportunity for me to use some embedded suggestions for myself. When I picture this beautiful nature scene in Big Sur, I always think positive thoughts about myself. This is a good time for me to reaffirm how much I love myself and how much I accept myself for who I am.

As we relax through these visualizations, they take on a deeper meaning that truly penetrates our soul. We should all visualize regularly. It is not only beautiful and peaceful, but it can be rewarding as well.

Karen Blaine is a professional, certified hypnotherapist from the International association of Professional Conversational Hypnotherapists. She specializes in conversational hypnotherapy. This kind of therapy allows the conscious mind to integrate more fully with the subconscious.

Karen is dedicated and devoted to helping others. Hypnotherapy for her it is a labor of love. She is very passionate about what her chosen profession, and strives to continually learn from others.

Karen graduated from California State University, Northridge (CSUN) with an undergraduate degree in speech-communications. She has lived in Southern California all of her life. She raised four wonderful children who have grown into positive, caring and successful adults.

Please contact her by e-mail *kbhypnotherapy@gmail.com.* The website is *kbhypnotherapy.com*

Karen Blaine
IAPCH certified hypnotherapist

phone: (805) 630-4150
email: kbhypnotherapy@gmail.com
web: www.kbhypnotherapy.com

PROFESSIONAL • TRUSTWORTHY • PROVEN RESULTS